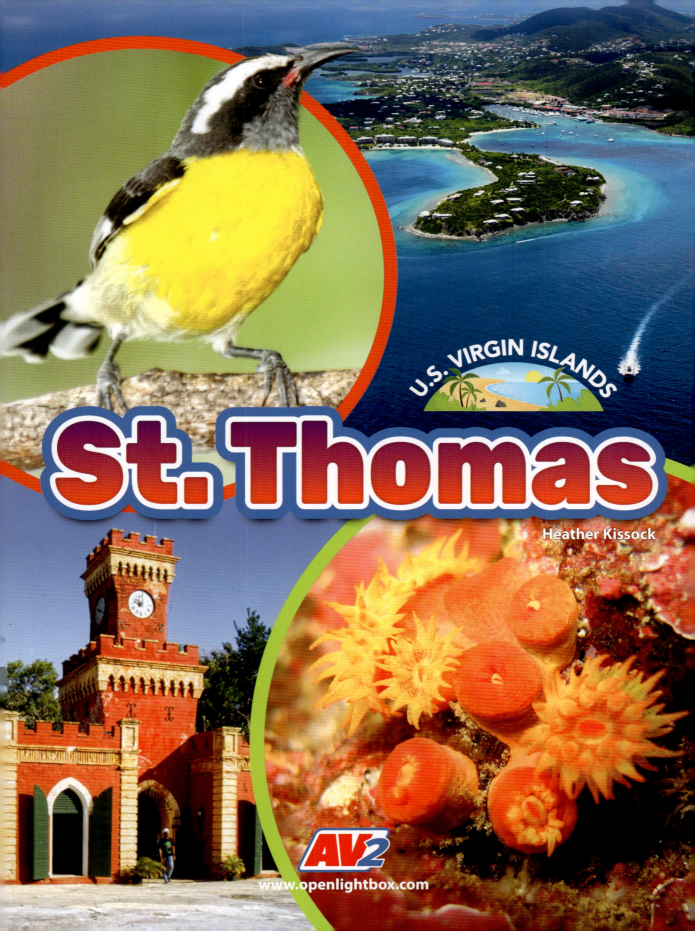
U.S. VIRGIN ISLANDS
St. Thomas
Heather Kissock

AV2
www.openlightbox.com

Step 1
Go to www.openlightbox.com

Step 2
Enter this unique code

NVEKD1DE3

Step 3
Explore your interactive eBook!

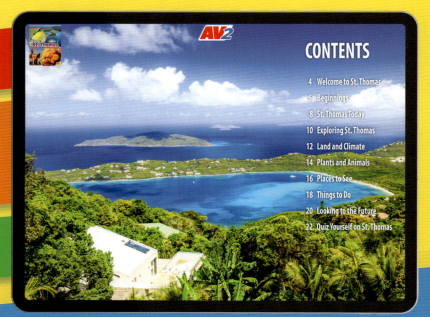

AV2 is optimized for use on any device

Your interactive eBook comes with...

Contents
Browse a live contents page to easily navigate through resources

Audio
Listen to sections of the book read aloud

Videos
Watch informative video clips

Weblinks
Gain additional information for research

Slideshows
View images and captions

Try This!
Complete activities and hands-on experiments

Key Words
Study vocabulary, and complete a matching word activity

Quizzes
Test your knowledge

Share
Share titles within your Learning Management System (LMS) or Library Circulation System

Citation
Create bibliographical references following APA, CMOS, and MLA styles

This title is part of our AV2 digital subscription

1-Year Grades K–5 Subscription
ISBN 978-1-7911-3320-7

Access hundreds of AV2 titles with our digital subscription. Sign up for a FREE trial at www.openlightbox.com/trial

The digital components of this book are guaranteed to stay active for at least five years from the date of publication.

U.S. VIRGIN ISLANDS

St. Thomas

CONTENTS

- 2 Interactive eBook Code
- 4 Welcome to St. Thomas
- 6 Beginnings
- 8 St. Thomas Today
- 10 Exploring St. Thomas
- 12 Land and Climate
- 14 Plants and Animals
- 16 Places to See
- 18 Things to Do
- 20 Looking to the Future
- 22 Quiz Yourself on St. Thomas
- 23 Key Words/Index

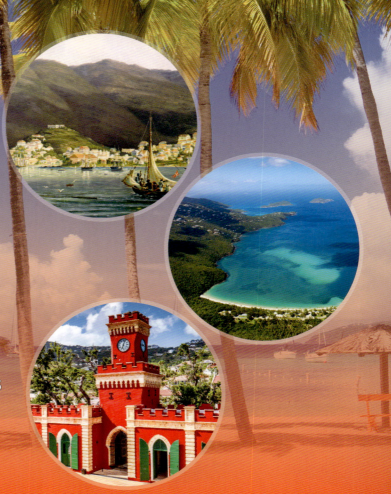

WELCOME TO
St. Thomas

St. Thomas has **more than 40** white-sand beaches.

Charlotte Amalie is St. Thomas's **only** town.

St. Thomas has the **largest airport** and **cruise ship port** in the U.S. Virgin Islands.

4 U.S. Virgin Islands

The Caribbean Sea is known for its many islands. The U.S. Virgin Islands lie in the eastern Caribbean, about 1,100 miles (1,770 kilometers) south of Florida. They are called the U.S. Virgin Islands because they are a **territory** of the United States. More than 50 islands make up this territory. The three largest are St. Croix, St. John, and St. Thomas.

St. Thomas is the most northwest of these main islands. It is home to the territory's capital, Charlotte Amalie. As a center for business and tourism, St. Thomas is more **cosmopolitan** than the other islands. While guests come to enjoy its warm waters and white-sand beaches, they can also stay in luxurious resorts, eat at elegant restaurants, and shop in high-end stores.

St. Thomas

Beginnings

St. Thomas was millions of years in the making. Its formation started when the **tectonic plates** that lie beneath the Caribbean Sea collided with each other. This movement caused underwater volcanoes to erupt, sending **molten** rock to the water's surface. As the rock cooled, it merged into a mass that eventually became the island of St. Thomas.

Christopher Columbus was on his second voyage to the New World when he came upon St. Thomas. His first voyage had taken place the year before.

People did not appear on St. Thomas until about 1500 BC. It is believed that these first inhabitants were seasonal residents who came to the island to fish. The first permanent settlers arrived sometime between 300 and 100 BC. These people were the Arawak, an **Indigenous** people from South America. They lived on the island until the mid-15th century AD, when they were replaced by another Indigenous group known as the Carib.

In 1493, European explorer Christopher Columbus visited St. Thomas while sailing through the area. He did not encourage settlement there, so the island remained relatively undeveloped. Over the years, it became a haven for pirates. However, in 1672, St. Thomas was made a **colony** of Denmark. The Danish used the island mainly for sugar production. By 1865, the United States was expressing an interest in buying St. Thomas, St. John, and St. Croix. The country finally gained possession of the islands in 1917.

By the mid-1800s, Charlotte Amalie was a center for transatlantic trade, with ships from various countries docking in its harbor to deliver and pick up cargo.

U.S. Virgin Islands

St. Thomas Timeline

1500 BC
People begin coming to St. Thomas to fish in its waters.

100 BC
The Arawak are living on the island year-round.

1493 AD
Christopher Columbus encounters St. Thomas while exploring the area.

1657
The Dutch set up a post on St. Thomas.

1671
The Danish lay claim to St. Thomas. Charlotte Amalie, named after a Danish queen, is founded the following year.

1700s
St. Thomas becomes a center for the **slave trade**. Slavery is not abolished on the island until 1848.

1917
The United States purchases St. Thomas, St. John, and St. Croix from the Danish for $25 million.

2023
Icon of the Seas, the world's largest cruise ship, docks at St. Thomas during her maiden voyage.

St. Thomas 7

St. Thomas Today

Approximately 42,000 people call St. Thomas home. This is almost 50 percent of the entire U.S. Virgin Islands population. Most of St. Thomas's residents live in the central part of the island. This is where Charlotte Amalie is located.

People of African **descent** make up about 90 percent of St. Thomas's population. The island also has people with Spanish, Portuguese, British, French, and Puerto Rican backgrounds. English is the most common language heard on St. Thomas. Other languages spoken there include French and Spanish.

Charlotte Amalie's Main Street is known as one of the top shopping areas in the Caribbean. It features both familiar chain stores as well as locally owned shops.

More than **2 million tourists** visit St. Thomas every year.

The average cost of a house on St. Thomas is **$485,000**.

St. Thomas's residents make an average of **$58,000** per year. That works out to **$28 per hour**.

8 U.S. Virgin Islands

Tourism is the island's main industry. Many of St. Thomas's residents work in tourism-related jobs. Some, such as tour guides, may work solely with tourists. Others, including restaurant servers, may serve both tourists and locals.

In 2020, approximately 17 percent of St. Thomas's working population was employed in the hospitality industry. This includes restaurant servers.

Exploring St. Thomas

The second largest of the U.S. Virgin Islands, St. Thomas stretches 13 miles (21 km) long and 4 miles (6.4 km) wide. The island covers an area of 32 square miles (83 square km). Its closest neighbor is St. John, which lies about 3 miles (5 km) east. St. Croix is located about 40 miles (64 km) south of both islands. The U.S. territory of Puerto Rico is approximately the same distance to the west of St. Thomas.

Charlotte Amalie

Charlotte Amalie is the only town in the U.S. Virgin Islands with more than 10,000 people. Its population currently stands at about 14,500. While Charlotte Amalie is known for its modern conveniences, remnants of its Danish past can still be seen. Several buildings from this era remain in the town.

Crown Mountain

Crown Mountain is the highest point on St. Thomas and all the U.S. Virgin Islands. It rises to a height of 1,556 feet (474 meters). A hiking trail leads to the summit.

Magens Bay

Located on the northern coast of St. Thomas, Magens Bay is known for its horseshoe-shaped shoreline, turquoise waters, and white-sand beaches. The bay is surrounded by a **nature reserve**. People can walk the Discover Nature Trail to and from Magens Bay to experience a variety of **ecosystems**, ranging from **mangrove** swamps to tropical forests.

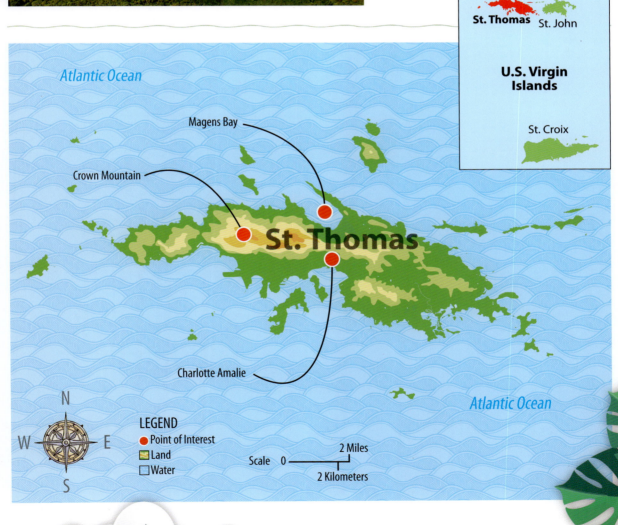

St. Thomas | 11

Land and Climate

St. Thomas is a very hilly island with only a few flat areas. The main ridge of mountains runs east–west. Several other hills branch off from this ridge. Some extend right to the water's edge, helping to form the island's rugged coastline.

Forests cover more than 50 percent of St. Thomas. The island has both tropical and subtropical forests, although most are the latter. Mangroves are found on the east-central part of the island, where they are protected within a nature reserve. Many of St. Thomas's original forests were removed when Europeans first arrived to make room for their settlements. Programs are now in place to restore more tree cover to the island.

St. Thomas is surrounded by several small islands and cays. Most are uninhabited, with many considered to be wildlife reserves.

Salt water surrounds St. Thomas, but the island holds very few freshwater resources. Rivers and streams sometimes form during the island's rainy season, when water starts running down its hills. Small **aquifers** also lie underground. However, neither of these resources supply enough water for regular use. Most of St. Thomas's water must be brought in from Puerto Rico. Some residents also collect rainwater.

St. Thomas receives about 50 inches (127 centimeters) of rain over the course of the year. Most of this falls between May and November. Due to its proximity to the equator, temperatures, on average, typically stay around 80° Fahrenheit (27° Celsius) year-round. Like other Caribbean islands, St. Thomas is vulnerable to hurricanes. These normally occur between the months of June and November.

Average High Temperatures

JAN	82°F (28°C)
FEB	82°F (28°C)
MAR	82°F (28°C)
APR	84°F (29°C)
MAY	86°F (30°C)
JUN	88°F (31°C)
JUL	88°F (31°C)
AUG	88°F (31°C)
SEP	88°F (31°C)
OCT	88°F (31°C)
NOV	86°F (30°C)
DEC	84°F (29°C)

In 2017, Hurricane Irma tore through St. Thomas, causing widespread damage to property.

St. Thomas

Plants and Animals

St. Thomas's warm climate provides **habitat** for numerous plants and animals. Tropical flowers and trees grow throughout St. Thomas. A wide variety of **mammals**, birds, **reptiles**, and other creatures also make their home on the island.

Flamboyant Tree

The brilliant red-orange flowers of the flamboyant tree add splashes of color to St. Thomas's hills. The trees can grow to a height of 40 feet (12 m), while their flowers can measure up to 4 inches (10 centimeters) across. The flamboyant is in bloom from May to September.

Manchineel

The manchineel is considered the most dangerous tree in the U.S. Virgin Islands. Its fruit, which looks like an apple, is poisonous and can lead to death when consumed. Touching its sap can cause burns. Typically found near beach areas, the tree can be identified by its shiny, rounded leaves.

14 U.S. Virgin Islands

Magnificent Frigatebird

Magnificent frigatebirds can often be seen soaring along St. Thomas's coastline. These large seabirds rarely flap their wings, relying instead on **thermals** to keep aloft. Males have a bright red pouch on their throat. They inflate this pouch when trying to attract a mate.

Blue Land Crab

Blue land crabs live throughout the U.S. Virgin Islands and the Caribbean in general. They are mostly found within 5 miles (8 km) of the shoreline. These crabs come in a variety of blues, ranging from dark blue to a pale grayish blue. They can measure up to 6 inches (15 cm) across and weigh more than 18 ounces (500 grams).

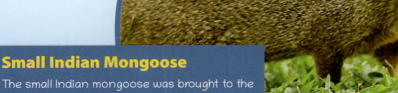

Small Indian Mongoose

The small Indian mongoose was brought to the U.S. Virgin Islands in the late 19th century as a form of rat control. It now helps to keep the region's snake population in line. Mongooses live in a variety of habitats on St. Thomas, ranging from coastal areas to forests.

Places to See

There is much to see in St. Thomas. Historic sites provide guests with an understanding and appreciation of the Caribbean people. Scenic viewpoints allow tourists to relax and enjoy their visit.

St. Thomas is a popular destination for cruise ships. The island sees approximately 1.7 million visitors arrive by ship every year.

Charlotte Amalie has many of the island's top attractions. History buffs who also enjoy a workout can climb the city's 99 Steps, which were built by the Danish in the 18th century to help people navigate St. Thomas's hilly terrain. The steps lead to an old watchtower now known as Blackbeard's Castle. Named after a famous pirate, the building serves as a showcase for pirate history. Government House is situated near the foot of the 99 Steps. Built in 1867, it was where the Danish government's representatives met. Today, it serves as the office of the island's governor.

Palm trees and flowers have been planted along the sides of the 99 Steps to provide color and shade.

The St. Thomas Synagogue is **one** of **only five** synagogues in the world to have sand on its floor.

St. Thomas's **99 Steps** actually number **103**.

Fort Christian was named a U.S. National Historic Site in **1997**.

16 U.S. Virgin Islands

Fort Christian is the oldest standing structure in the U.S. Virgin Islands. Built almost 350 years ago, it has served as a government building, a place of worship, and a prison at different times in its history. Today, the fort houses the St. Thomas Museum, which highlights the history of both the fort and the island.

Fort Christian was built between 1672 and 1678. It was named after the Danish king, Christian V, who ruled from 1670 to 1699.

St. Thomas's natural scenery is just as fascinating as its history. Many of the island's best viewpoints are found at high elevations. Mountain Top is often touted as St. Thomas's most popular tourist attraction. Situated on St. Peter Mountain, it provides views of Magens Bay. Located off one of St. Thomas's main roads, Drake's Seat overlooks the north side of the island and on to the **British Virgin Islands**. The viewpoint is named after explorer Sir Francis Drake, but it is unclear if he was ever actually there.

Cable cars take guests from St. Thomas Harbor to the top of Paradise Point, where they can look out over Charlotte Amalie and the harbor itself. On clear days, the view can be extended to include the islands of Puerto Rico and St. Croix.

Things to Do

A wide range of activities awaits visitors to St. Thomas. As it is an island, water fun is at the top of the list. However, people can also participate in a number of land adventures. For those who enjoy cultural pursuits, festivals and celebrations are held in St. Thomas throughout the year.

With warm waters year-round, St. Thomas is a popular place for snorkeling. Those who venture underwater are likely to encounter a variety of sea life, including dolphins, sea turtles, and stingrays. For people wanting a deeper experience, a trip to the Coral World Ocean Park is a must. Its sea trek experience allows guests to walk on the ocean floor while wearing an oxygen-filled helmet.

Taking a walk along the harbor is a popular pastime for tourists visiting St. Thomas.

Coral World Ocean Park provides visitors with the opportunity to interact with sea turtles and other aquatic creatures.

18 U.S. Virgin Islands

There are many ways to explore St. Thomas's hills and valleys. Hiking trails wind past natural wonders such as tidal pools, volcanic cliffs, and **blowholes**. Jeep tours take people over the bumps and dips of hidden back-country trails. To get an elevated view of the island, visitors can go ziplining over the treetops or parasailing above the sea.

Parasailing tours offer guests a bit of adventure and a unique way to see the island.

To experience Caribbean culture, there is no better time to visit St. Thomas than during Carnival. Held in April and May, the festival pays tribute to the island's history and traditions. Guests are treated to parades, pageants, **calypso** shows, street dances, tasty food, and much more.

Elaborate costumes are a big part of St. Thomas's Carnival parade, which takes place on a 2-mile (3.2-km) route through Charlotte Amalie's downtown.

Looking to the Future

Recent years have seen population decline throughout the U.S. Virgin Islands. In 2010, St. Thomas had 51,634 residents. In just 14 years, the island has had about an 18 percent drop in population. St. Thomas is already feeling the impact of this decrease. Some jobs, for instance, are becoming difficult to fill.

There are several reasons for the population decline. Many people are leaving St. Thomas to move to the U.S. mainland, where they see more opportunities for personal and professional growth. Some left after Hurricane Irma devastated the island in 2017, deciding to rebuild their lives somewhere else. Since the hurricane, the cost of living has risen in St. Thomas. This has made it more difficult for people to live there.

In 2023, only about 19 percent of the population in the U.S. Virgin Islands was under the age of 15.

St. Thomas's weather has been taken into consideration when planning new housing developments. To avoid the damage sustained by some of the island's older homes, hurricane-resistant and energy-independent features are now included in design plans.

Community leaders have been developing a plan to encourage St. Thomas's residents to stay on the island. Affordable housing units are being built to provide low-income families with comfortable homes. Local schools are introducing programs that will allow people to advance their learning without moving to the mainland. Steps are also being taken to make the island better able to withstand severe storms. It is hoped that, with these improvements, more people will decide to make St. Thomas their permanent home.

PROBLEM SOLVER

Plans are in place to make St. Thomas a safe and welcoming place to live. What other actions could local leaders take to encourage people to remain on or move to the island?

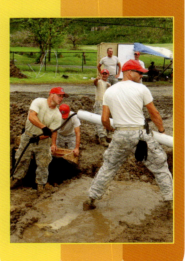

St. Thomas 21

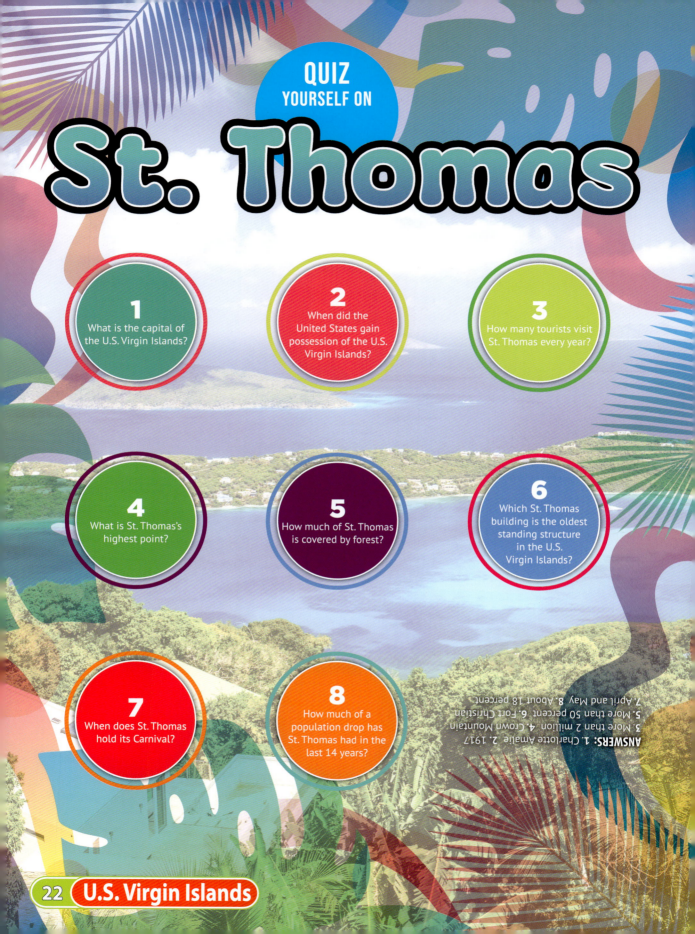

QUIZ YOURSELF ON St. Thomas

1 What is the capital of the U.S. Virgin Islands?

2 When did the United States gain possession of the U.S. Virgin Islands?

3 How many tourists visit St. Thomas every year?

4 What is St. Thomas's highest point?

5 How much of St. Thomas is covered by forest?

6 Which St. Thomas building is the oldest standing structure in the U.S. Virgin Islands?

7 When does St. Thomas hold its Carnival?

8 How much of a population drop has St. Thomas had in the last 14 years?

ANSWERS: 1. Charlotte Amalie 2. 1917 3. More than 2 million 4. Crown Mountain 5. More than 50 percent 6. Fort Christian 7. April and May 8. About 18 percent.

22 U.S. Virgin Islands

Key Words

aquifers: layers of underground rock that contain water or allow water to pass

blowholes: holes in the ground that jets of water shoot out of

British Virgin Islands: a group of Caribbean islands that form a territory of the United Kingdom

calypso: a lively musical style from the Caribbean

colony: a country or area under the control of another country

cosmopolitan: composed of people from or at home in many parts of the world

descent: the background of a person in terms of family origin

ecosystems: communities of living organisms that live and interact with each other in a specific environment

habitat: the natural environment of an animal, plant, or other organism

Indigenous: relating to a country's original, or native, people

mammals: animals that have hair or fur and feed their young milk

mangrove: a tropical tree, found near water, whose roots grow partly above ground

molten: something transformed into a liquid state due to intense heat

nature reserve: an area that has been set aside to protect the animals and plants that live on it

reptiles: cold-blooded animals that have a backbone and a body that is covered with scales

slave trade: the buying and selling of human beings, especially African people, from the 16th to the 19th century

tectonic plates: large slabs of rock that make up the surface of Earth

territory: an organized division of a country that is not yet admitted to the full rights of a state

thermals: upward currents of air

99 Steps 16

animals 14, 15, 18
Arawak 6, 7

Blackbeard's Castle 16

Carib 6
Caribbean Sea 5, 6
Carnival 19, 22
Charlotte Amalie 4, 5, 6, 7, 8, 10, 11, 16, 17, 19, 22
Columbus, Christopher 6, 7
Crown Mountain 10, 11, 22

Denmark 6, 7
Drake's Seat 17

forests 11, 12, 15, 22
Fort Christian 16, 17, 22

Government House 16

hiking 10, 19
hurricanes 13, 20, 21

jeep tours 19

language 8

Magens Bay 11, 17
Mountain Top 17

pirates 6, 16,
population 8, 9, 10, 20, 21, 22
Puerto Rico 10, 13, 17

settlers 6, 12
snorkeling 18
St. Croix 5, 6, 7, 10, 11, 17
St. John 5, 6, 7, 10, 11

tourism 5, 8, 9, 16, 17, 18, 22

Get the best of both worlds.

AV2 bridges the gap between print and digital.

The expandable resources toolbar enables quick access to content including **videos**, **audio**, **activities**, **weblinks**, **slideshows**, **quizzes**, and **key words**.

Animated videos make static images come alive.

Resource icons on each page help readers to further **explore key concepts**.

Published by Lightbox Learning Inc.
276 5th Avenue
Suite 704 #917
New York, NY 10001
Website: www.openlightbox.com

Copyright ©2026 Lightbox Learning Inc.
All rights reserved. No part of this publication may be reproduced, stored in a retrieval system, or transmitted in any form or by any means, electronic, mechanical, photocopying, recording, or otherwise, without the prior written permission of the publisher.

Library of Congress Cataloging-in-Publication Data
Names: Kissock, Heather, author.
Title: St. Thomas / Heather Kissock.
Other titles: Saint Thomas
Description: New York, NY : Lightbox Learning Inc., 2026. | Series: U.S. Virgin Islands | Includes index. | Audience: Grades 2-3
Identifiers: LCCN 2024047655 (print) | LCCN 2024047656 (ebook) | ISBN 9798874507343 (library binding) | ISBN 9798874511555 (paperback) | ISBN 9798874507350 (ebook other) | ISBN 9798874507374 (ebook other)
Subjects: LCSH: Saint Thomas (United States Virgin Islands : Island)--Juvenile literature.
Classification: LCC F2105 .K57 2026 (print) | LCC F2105 (ebook) | DDC 917.297/22--dc23/eng/20241214
LC record available at https://lccn.loc.gov/2024047655
LC ebook record available at https://lccn.loc.gov/2024047656

Printed in Guangzhou, China
1 2 3 4 5 6 7 8 9 0 29 28 27 26 25

032025
101124

Project Coordinator: Heather Kissock
Designer: Terry Paulhus

Photo Credits
Every reasonable effort has been made to trace ownership and to obtain permission to reprint copyright material. The publisher would be pleased to have any errors or omissions brought to its attention so that they may be corrected in subsequent printings. The publisher acknowledges Getty Images, Alamy, Bridgeman Images, Minden Pictures, and Shutterstock as its primary image suppliers for this title.